CW00660969

SPIRIT OF
THE NEW FOREST

MIKE READ

First published in Great Britain in 2007. Reprinted 2010

Copyright © 2007 Mike Read

British Library Cataloguing-in-Publication Data
A CIP record for this title is available from the British Library

ISBN 978 0 85710 002 3

PiXZ Books
Halsgrove House, Ryelands Industrial Estate,
Bagley Road, Wellington, Somerset TA21 9PZ
Tel: 01823 653777
Fax: 01823 216796
email: sales@halsgrove.com

An imprint of Halstar Ltd, part of the Halsgrove group
of companies Information on all Halsgrove titles is
available at: www.halsgrove.com

Printed and bound in China by Toppan Leefung Printing Ltd

Introduction

With a history stretching back over 900 years to the time of William the Conquerer, the New Forest is a truly fabulous place, containing habitats that range from bogs and heathlands through to ancient and ornamental woodlands. The area boasts exceptional scenery and a huge variety of wildlife (although perhaps it is best known for its ponies). The vast tracts of heathland, a blaze of purple in late summer, take on an exciting new facet as autumn mists or winter frosts give them a quite different look. In springtime, the bright-yellow blossoms of the gorse flag up the birth of a fresh season.

Come rain or shine, mist or howling gale, by finding the quieter spots in the New Forest it is possible to become at one with nature. As it says on one particular seat in the Forest: 'Sit still, look long and hold yourself quiet.' Then you'll find that the Forest will come to you.

Ancient beech in autumn
The timing and quality of the best autumn colours varies from
one year to another and depends very much on the weather.
This is a beech at its very best.

Snow among ancient trees
The rays of light indicate hope that the three-month-long freeze-up
of the 1962/63 winter is not about to return.

Fall colours
Beech leaves cling to slender twigs before adding to the deepening autumn carpet below.

Opposite page:
Winter sunrise over Strodgemoor Bottom
Frost covers the ground in a boggy area, where snipe may feed in winter and curlews nest in spring.

Pony beside beech tree
The warmth of the sun in this sheltered glade
is much appreciated after a cold night.

Opposite page:
Pines and light rays, Cranes Moor

Reflected oaks
The stillness of the Ober Water provides an ideal reflective surface to add to this special moment.

Opposite page:
Sunrise over Fletchers Green
Mist and low cloud threatened to mask the sunrise but, in the end, all of the elements combined to provide a fabulous scene.

**Sweet chestnut bark,
Wilverley Inclosure**

**Sweet chestnut leaves
in dappled light**

Opposite page:
**Sweet chestnut,
Backley Inclosure**

Light ray in Broomy Inclosure
Following a cold, still night it was obvious that there would be
mist in the early morning. All that was needed was for the
camera to be in the right place as the sun broke through…

Oak and beech in Berry Beeches

So often woodlands can be of a single species but here we
see the New Forest's best two broadleaved trees together.

A prickly meal!
This pony instinctively knows the nutritional value
of gorse, but has to nibble very carefully.

Opposite page:
Old grey mare at sunrise
After a health check and the payment of appropriate fees, most of the breeding stock
of ponies will be returned to the open Forest, following the autumn 'drifts' or round-ups.

Silver birches reflected
Recent rains conveniently
provided some rather large
puddles to help make
this wonderful picture.

Opposite page:
**Autumn colours
in Berry Wood**

Silver birch at Soarley Bottom

Almost cloudless skies contrast beautifully with the autumn tones of this fine tree.

Opposite page:

Blooming gorse above Vales Moor

In the spring, flowering gorse bushes add a vibrant splash of colour on otherwise dull-looking heaths.

20

Beech branches in spring

As the days lengthen and we lose the coldness of winter, buds swell and burst to welcome the spring.

Beech leaves and trunks
The stark contrast between dark bark and bright-green leaves tell of the season of promise; spring has arrived.

Beech blooms
Once the leaves offer some protection from April showers, flowers bloom and are pollinated to produce the beech mast.

Coniferous plantation
Light spills into the woodland floor, where bracken provides somewhere for the deer to hide during daylight hours.

Opposite page:
Ponies on Rockford Common
A mare and her young foal push through the bracken, heading for her favoured feeding ground.

Left:
Cross-leaved heath

Below:
Bell heather

Opposite page:
Ling or common heather
By far the most widespread of
the Forest's heathers, this one
usually blooms a little later
than the other two.

Pony in snow, Linwood
This pony has a long, thick coat to help keep
it warm during the coldest months.

Opposite page:
Mare and foal on Whitefield Moor

Telegraph poles of the future?

Serried ranks of Scots pines grow as a valuable timber crop in South Oakley Inclosure.

Felled Scots pines, Highland Water Inclosure

Timber production is an important part of the New Forest's daily life. These logs await collection and transportation to the sawmills.

Avon Water stream
Near Wootton Coppice Inclosure, shadows of oak trunks
break up the sun's reflection on the water.

Opposite page:
Sunset over Rockford Common

Moonrise over Appleslade Inclosure
As the sun sets, a full moon rises in the opposite direction.

Opposite page:
Scots pine at sunset
The brightness of the sun throws these pines into silhouette and emphasises how they vary in shape.

New Forest pony, Hincheslea Moor
A pony gazes across the heathland as mist rises in the distance.

Seize the light
Light rays spill from behind this pony, photographed early on an autumn day.

How are the mighty fallen
Gales can wreak havoc, especially on trees weakened by age and disease, but this is just the beginning of the important decay process as insects and fungi now set to work.

Fallen leaves
The rich brown of beech and sweet chestnut leaves contrast with the mosses on the woodland floor.

Opposite page:
Pollarded beech, Vinney Ridge

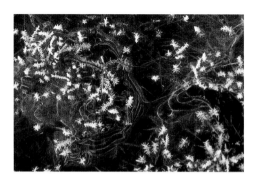

Ice on a drained puddle
When frost quickly follows rain in areas which are free-draining, the surface freezes but beneath the water drains away, leaving these very brittle ice patterns.

Gorse with hoar-frost
As the setting sun gains a touch of colour, the hoar-frost on this sprig of gorse seems to be glowing orange-yellow.

Sunrise over Puckpits Inclosure

Red deer near Brockenhurst
While most of the herd rest, there are always one or two on 'sentry duty'.

Fallow deer on Ridley Plain
This fine buck watches over resting fallow does during the autumn rut.

Sunlit bracken
Low rays strike bracken tops
through a gap at the edge
of the Forest. Later, the
whole Forest floor will be
bathed in sunlight.

Opposite page:
Beeches and bracken
Sun rakes through the
early-morning mist like
cold fingers holding up
this leaning tree.

Pigs at pannage, Fritham

During the autumn, acorns fall from the oaks and could prove poisonous to ponies and cattle. Pigs can, however, eat them with impunity, hence the traditional 'pannage' season.

Opposite page:
Pony at sunrise

Golden mist surrounds this pony as the sun imparts warmth to a new day.

In Knightwood Inclosure
A grassy pathway leads past the warm-coloured trunks, birches and bracken and takes you into the dense conifers, where deer may be lying-up for the day.

Imposing beauty
With a little help from Man who pollarded (beheaded!) such trees,
Nature has provided a magnificent scene for the camera.

Simple is best
An angled tree base, some tinted bracken and a little
mist is all that is needed to make an image;
sometimes simplicity makes the picture.

Opposite page:
Beech trunks and holly
These trees are growing along the side of the Bolderwood
ornamental drive, but most people don't give them a second glance.

Fallow deer at Bolderwood Deer Sanctuary

In summer the fallow deer have beautiful speckled coats, though there are exceptions such as white or mostly black individuals.

Ponies graze on Whitefield Moor
A peaceful scene as a mare and her foal graze towards the woods along the Ober Water.

Rising moon near Burley
It is said that we get more
clear skies around the time of
a full moon than any other
part of the lunar cycle.

Opposite page:
Sunset over Long Pond
The red clouds reflected
by the still water surface
add a special depth
to this image.

Sunset over Whitten Pond

The sun has just disappeared over the horizon yet it still lights the rims of the clouds above.

Beaulieu estuary

Great spotted woodpecker

Decaying timber is often home for a range of insects and their larvae, hence the woodpecker's constant attention to places like this.

Opposite page:
Brock emerges

As dusk falls over the Forest, nocturnal species of wildlife begin their activities. Here a badger leaves its sett to search for tasty morsels, such as beetles and earthworms.

Oak planter
Jays collect acorns when there is a glut in the autumn.
They bury them for consumption during leaner times,
but of course not all of them are found again.

Palace House, Beaulieu
The view across the Mill Pond at Beaulieu is quintessentially English.

Tranquil woodlands
On a day such as this, the smells of the woodland fill
your nostrils as the sunlight brings warmth.

Evening skies over Hatchet Pond

Side-lit young beeches
A scene from Parkhill Inclosure, where mid-winter frost lingers beyond stately young trunks.